Burnin' From Within

A Teenagers' Struggle

by
Traci Gaines

authorHOUSE™

1663 LIBERTY DRIVE, SUITE 200
BLOOMINGTON, INDIANA 47403
(800) 839-8640
WWW.AUTHORHOUSE.COM

First published by AuthorHouse 05/18/05

ISBN: 1-4208-4766-X (sc)

Library of Congress Control Number: 2005903177

Printed in the United States of America
Bloomington, Indiana

This book is printed on acid-free paper.

Acknowledgements

I would like to thank all the teenagers that I have been around, or have had the chance to talk to. I have known some wonderful teenagers in my life. I have known some teenagers that have inspired me. I know some teenagers that I have literally watched grow up. Sorry to say I have had to see a few of them make their way to see the Lord. I would like to thank God for letting me have the opportunity to work with kids from pre-school, up to teenage. I have seen the children go through so much just on a day-to-day basis, and that is why I chose to write this book.

Table Of Topics

These are just some of the topics in the book. I ask that you read the book all the way through to get an idea of all the topics that I speak of. Discuss them with your teen, or just a friend. The topics may get to you, they may bore you, but they are here for you to notice. I always feel there is a need to talk about the things that most people want to keep under raps. Topics are ususally that way for a reason. Hopefully you will enjoy this book also. I thankyou for taking the time to pay attention!

Foreward by Traci Gaines

When I first decided to write this book I thought about some of the teenagers I deal with on a daily basis. I thought about how I grew up with my mom, and wondering what my children have to go through as teenagers. I know in this day and time teenagers have to fight the drug game, gangs, and supposed friends. The world is a wonderful and harsh place. Let's be real here, I know so many horror stories about things that I've heard teenagers going through on a daily basis it's scary. Let alone just getting up in the morning, I guess maybe they feel like they have to go to war right here in the hood. I know some days are good, but there are the bad days too and hopefully they can deal with it.

Introduction

This book is for all of the adults and teenagers who may be going through a lot of different stages. I know that I have been through a lot being a parent. Hopefully this will help some of the teenagers to figure out what they need to do to occupy their time, while they wait to become adults.

I know how hard it is to be a teen. I used to be one myself, and it was hard. There were times when I had to go in my room and cry to myself I was so mad at what my mom was doing to me. It was so good at times, like when I had my first birthday at 18. I always laugh because they only played a song called Battaram that the kids would dance to. I remeber wanting to wear certain clothes to school. I remember we had crews back in the day. I remember doing things in high school that we weren't supposed to,not going to class,smoking weed, or whatever else we weren't supposed to do. I remember teen pregnancy,and dope dealers, and gangs. I remember learning how to drive and not being able to until I was 18. My mom didn't play that teend riving thing. I remember starting to learn what likeing boys were like. I remember learning about my body for the first time. I remember telling mom I was doing one thing and her driving down the street and catching me in a lie. I remember finding church for the first time. I remember being confused about it. I remember not going and going to the store instead. I remember being loves by friends, and also beign betrayed by friends. I remember making mistakes that I felt could only be done by me. I remember being the only girl who couldn't make it on the cheerleading team. I remember a friend of mine teasing me soo much that I didn't want to play basketball any more, and I was good at it. These are just some of the memories that I live with everyday. This is also why adults say,been there done that!

Burnin' From Within

There are some teenagers now that amaze me with the things they say and do. Which I'm sure everyone can agree with this fact. The teenagers now a days have to go through a lot. They have to deal with going to school everyday. They have to deal with not going to school everyday. They have to deal with each other as far as communication. They talk to each other, but some of them don't like the topic of conversation. The girls have to deal with each other as far as who likes which boy. They have to deal with the fact that they may not like a group of girls, or even one girl for that fact. They have to deal with the boys constant sexual harrasment, or just if their friends. The boys have to deal with which click, or crew as we used to call it back in the day, they want to be in. They have to worry about who's the man. They have to deal with becoming a man and they have to worry about the gangs that are in the neighborhood. They all have to worry about the dope game. They all have to worry about growing up with their parents nagging them all the time. They have to worry about hanging out and not getting into any trouble.

There are some teenagers who are going to school to try to get good grades. There are some who are struggling to get good grades. There is a school that rewards the students that get good grades, with certificates. The other students who aren't getting good grades get a bike as a reward. This leads the other children who are doing the right thing, in the wrong direction. I've seen it happen, but the children don't improve their grades, they continue to spiral downward. Then they tend to start all hanging together,with the same children that have bad grades.

There are some teachers who display the childrens work on the boards. There are some children that get d's and f's. This is a good display to hopefully get the children who have the lower grades, to improve. The only thing that seems to get the children to improve is there parent coming in to see what it is their actually doing all day.

The biggest problem in the schools today is the childrens attitudes. There are some that are very direspectful. They curse at the teacher. They talk back with no problem whatsoever. They do not have any respect for any grownups at all. They curse so often that people get tired of saying don't say things like that. They will sit up there and say things about the teacher, if she's old or funny looking. They use the same thing that they say for each other.

Another problem in the schools is that the teenagers, sorry to say, are having sexual intercourse. You can hear them talking about it with one another, and at times they'll try to say things in confidence to another friend. Kids just don't know that having intercourse at a young age is illegal and they can go to jail. One way is when the young man is older than the girl. He doesn't know it and he gets in trouble for having intercourse with her. The other way of course is an older man having intercourse with a young girl. That is called statutory rape. As far as sexual harassment goes, the girls tease the boys, and the boys tease the girls. It happens so much that the kids just usually shrug it off. They will tell someone some at the time, when someone is bothering them.

There are some children that think that school is not helping them at all. They feel that school has nothing to do with their regular life. They think that they can do what they want and that's not true. As black children in america, our children need to go to grade school. They need to finish high school. They need to continue on to college. Bill Cosby got in trouble for saying that blacks needed to be educated. It's true,nothing is going to happen as far as a good job unless we go onto college. There are some people that say they don't need college,that they can work and be happy. The only way this is good is if you stay on the same job for the rest of your life. If you switch from job to job,that's not good. If you quit jobs and try to lay on your behind all your life, it's not going to work. You try to hide from the world but you won't be able to function.

There are some people who try to vote no matter what happens. In Ohio the decideing vote came down to, alot of people who didn't vote. Out of the people that didn't vote, if twenty of them would have voted Kerry would have won. I vote because of all the trouble the slaves,civil rights, and who ever else fought for us to vote. I vote because I have the right to vote. I vote because I want to make a decision on what happens in california or for the united states.

There are some teenagers that think class time is play time. They talk all the time. They could talk the whole period now. The only time this changes is when parents or other people visit the class room. I have noticed though that it depends on which parent. I thought there was a difference in a male parent and a female. It depends on who the parent is. The kids choose which parent they want to be respectful for. The parents have come in and stated how they think a child usual acts,wild,talkative,smart,etc. I was told at one time while trying to teach the kids a lesson on George Washington Carver,that I was going to get cursed out. It's amazing to me that all the kids are trying to rebel, but their doing it in the wrong way.

There are some children that think they are supposed to have the latest clothes,shoes, and jewelery. I and other parents have believed in that old saying that a child only needs a shirt,pair of shoes, and coat on thier back in the winter time. I have heard children say to each other that one doesn't have the latest jordans, or other name brand tennis shoes. I have heard children talk about each other on the clothes that they have on. I have heard them talk about each other being poor. I have heard them put each other down on how much money their parents make. I have heard them talk about if the child doesn't have parents. All they worry about is what they are wearing. I know with most of them it's a style thing. Children are very cruel to each other.

There are some children who get into fights behind talking about someones mother. They tease about making love to the mother. They tease about how their parents look. They tease each other about how the parent dresses. They tease each other about what kind of house they live in. They don't understand how hard the parents work to give them what they have. They act as if they don't appreciate it.

There are some children that don't have older parents, their parents are younger. I am a young mother myself. I had my boys younger than some but still too young. There is a problem with older parents also. The teenagers don't respect their grandparents. There are some teenagers that are being raised by their grandparents. I know it's hard on the grandparents because they may not have the ability to spank the teenagers. The teenagers are so busy trying to be grown that they run around in circles trying to find themselves.

There are some teenagers that try to get into the dope game. They need to be careful because there are a lot of mean people out there. They are selling a product that can land them in jail. They have a need at times to do the drugs themselves and that will also land them in jail. The people who sell the dope at the highest level will hurt the one underneath them if they sell mor eof the product. If they can't find the person because their hiding they will find the nearest relative. They will make the most money and everyone underneath them will make less. Then when the person tries to stop or make a different life for themself they will be subject to being killed because they know too much about what is going on with the person in charge.

There are some kids who don't care if they go to juvenile hall. It is no joke. It is a smaller jail. You can only come out of your room at certain times. You can only eat certain foods. Your freedeom is gone. There are a whole bunch of people who are now in your life. There are the officers who deal with you on home arrest. There are probation officers that deal with you on home arrest. There are probation officers that deal with you on regular probation. There ar changes when you get off of probation. You have to deal with whatever crime you comitted for the rest of your life.

There are consequences that adults have to deal with out here in the real world also. You must obey the laws of speeding when driving. You are not supposed to drink and drive. When you so that you can get a DUI. You may possibly go to jail for man slaughter, if you are the driver in the wrong, and if you hit someone. Adults have to deal with fighting also,but if one person calls the police on the other,than one is going to jail. This is not a joke. This is not something that you want your parent to go through.

There are some teenagers that think killing an individual will get rid of their problems. This only causes more problems. The parents that take care of you and discipline you are there because GOD wanted them to be. GOD decides what teenagers are to bo with which parents. He has a reason for the parents and the teeanagers to be with each other. For those teenagers who don't believe in GOD, check into a church near you and talk to a pastor or priest to see what's going on with your life. Check around with other adults to see why you were put here on this earth. I recommend to anyone,take a look at the movie passion of the christ. My mom has always raised me on gospel music, she made me go to church. I continue to go to church now. I believe highly in GOD. I even prayed and told him that I will put him in each of my books to spread his word.

There are some teenagers that believe that just skating by the skin of your teeth is ok. The grade point average for all the teenagers is a 2.0. To me this is not good. Some children think that they can get a c average or even a d average a dn get by in life. I know that with black children they need to get a 3.0 average or better. They need to go to college. We don't have enough in this world as it is. We don't have black businesses anymore. My mom told me that when I was younger Oakland was mostly filled with black businesses. I remember being a teenager and going into different businesses. I saw all the black owners and I didn't know what it meant. Now that I see how everything is changed over to Asian and Latino businesses, I see the difference. Teenagers are the future and they need to go on to colleges start their own businesses. When that teenager comes around and needs a job you can be the one to give it to them.

There used to be a village that helped to raise teenagers back in the day. If I came home early, or if I had company over,there was a neighbor who let my mom know. A teenager couldn't get away with all the things that teenagers get away with now. If I was smoking weed and a neighbor saw me then they would tell my mom. If I was with a strange boy or man then they would tell my mom. These are some eaxamples of what used to happen back in the day. We had the problem of dope dealing back in the day too. I keep mentioning how we went to house parties and there was a possibility of a shooting then. Don't get me wrong I've heard stories of how some teenagers lived in the 66th village and there were shootings everyday. I have heard teenagers say that they saw a person get shot right in front of them. Whether it was a relative or not. These teenagers have gone through a lot.

There are some teenagers that go to the "urban schools". I don't like the word urban but it is here in this day and time. To me urban stands for poor and black. It's the schools where the parents can't afford to support the school. Now a days a lot of single parenting is present. I didn't believe that that was bad until my boys became teenagers. I have heard a lot of men say that they came out just find being raised only by their mother. I also know a lot of teenage boys and girls that are not focusing in school. They cannot be controlled to go the right way. There are teenagers who get in trouble with juvenile hall and the government says that it is due to not having a father around. Now in a way I feel they are listening to Tupacs' songs. He says he hates his dad because he was a coward and wasn't there.

There are a lot of teenagers who pay a lot of attention to this gangster rap. They pay close attention to the words. They think that shooting and killing is the answer. They also pay a lot of attention to the movies that are out that have become more sexually based in recent years. They play video games that bomb and destroy,shoot, and kill people. These are very deep issues that our teenagers are facing. If you try to keep them away from these things they will just go to their friends houses and play them. These things are making them become more violent minded. They know about combat and competition.

There are some teenagers now that gang up on one person at a time. There are some teeanagers that rob other teenagers. They go through a lot in a day and this is not something they want their parent to get involved in. The teenagers may not all like the one teenager,they get the teenager in a place where there a re no adults, and knock the crap out of the kid. There are some kids who literally have to go to school to make sure that they don't get jumped before the end of the day. I honked the horn twice at a groupof asian kids that were beating up on this black boy. I could not believe it. At one school I was told there is a fight at least once a day. I have heard of two incidents where a teacher has been attacked by teenagers, up to three at a time.

There are some parents who don't have any idea what their teenager is like when they aqre not around. The teenager will try to claim that they are an angel. Now that all this suing is going on, the teenagers are trying to use it to their advantage. They will tell the teacher that at times. They will continue to act up until their parent comes to the school. For that day they will act like an angel. They will not speak because it will incriminate them. I know now that it should be where all the parents should pop in to visit more than once out of the week to see what there teenager is doing. They will stop acting up,if the prinicpal is present. Some of them will not do it then. These teeanagers are very disrespectful and could care less what is going on or what is going on with their future.

There are some teeanagers who always keep their grades up. There are teenagers who are very afraid of their mom or dad. The teenagers that mostly keep themselves together are the caucasian kids and the teenagers with both parents. To me it goes right back to slavery days. The caucasian kids have had the education that they needed. The financial background that they needed. the living comfortable background that they needed to get where they are. The other thing they have is that the elementary school they went to education and financial support was provided. The middle school higher education and financial support has been provided. Then when the y go to high school, it's either catholic,private, or a higher education high school. There are some rich black parents that can provide this to their kids but that is the minority not the majority.

In slavery time blacks were not allowed to read. They were considered very ignorant and not qualified to read. Blacks were hung,dragged,limbs cut off, tortured, and abused behind trying to learn how to read. Slavery is still in the present,yes we have come far, but we have a long way to go. College is the answer now,but you can't get just any job even with a bachelors degree,from a four year college,now. If you don't go to college you are stuck at the bottom of the chain of command. You may be able to work your way up,but without a degree you can't make more pay or get a promotion. The system for having a degree now is changing to. You need a masters degree,two more years after your bachelors, to get a higher position. You must be able to know someone, this is called networking. I learned that word in college, and have used it to the best of my ability. This is another reason why BLACK TOWN would look so great. If we had our own banks, or own shopping malls, our own movie theaters, it would be wonderful. There have been people that say that black businesses get shut down. We still can't get loans that we are able to give back. We need young people to go to school to learn how to open their own business. We need instructers at possibly our own schools to teach our teenagers how to open their own business. I was told that when the atheletes,or actors, and actresses, get out there in stardom ville, they don't give back to the community.

There are some teenagers that act up on the buses. They try to tell the bus drivers to go faster. They curse at them. They all crowd in the back,like rosa parks,and Martin Luther King did all that for nothing. I sit in the front on purpose just because they did all that. Now I've noticed that the system has changed to where the elderly are allowed to sit in the very front or handicapped. The fare is $1.25 for adults, and 75 cents for teenagers. An adult pass is 60 dollars, and a youth pass is 15 dollars. That is very high. I remember when muni in San Francisco was 5 cents to ride. The teenagers need to realize now that they have cameras on the buses now, and again you can be taken to jail for hiting a bus driver.

There is another situation that is going on,it's called inlfation. It cost five dollars for two gallons of milk and a loaf of bread now. The food is getting more expensive now. Clothing is getting mor expensive now. Housing is getting more expensive now. Houses cost up to 400,000 dollars now. If the teenagers don't want to live in an apartment most of their life they need to go to college. Saving is very, very important. If you can save 5 dollars a day after one week you will have 25 dollars. After 4 weeks you will have 100 dollars. After 12 months you will have 1200 dollars. After12 years you will have 14,400 dollars. This is money that you can't touch. Later on you can use it for a down payment on a house or a car. Do not over use your credit. Get a credit card with a small amount on it, and only get one. Do not believe all the advertisements saying that a credit card will give you ten thousand dollars. They are going to go by your income that you make and it will end up being 1,000 dollars. Do not use one credit card to pay off another one. A good example of a credit card is american express. Once you charge 100 dollars, you must pay it back at the end of the month. I had a credit card and I would use it and pay it off as soon as I got the money. As soon as I stopped using it as much they cut off my using it. They eanted me to use it often and all the time. The last time I tooke my time paying it off, so they said it was out of use. So I paid it off and told them to cancel it.

There are teenagers that smoke weed,drink alcohol, smoke cocaine, and take ecstacy. I have seen lots of stories on tv and have heard about teenagers who have died from taking ecstacy. There have been teenage girls that have been date raped behind a date rape drug. I have heard about girls who are known as runners,where more than one boy has intercourse with her. All drugs do is enhance your thinking. It puts dopamine in your brain, and you think that everything is alright for a bout three hours. According to how long the drug takes affect on you, you may not be able to deal with the consequences until it's all over. In my experience either I didn't care when Iwas younger, the drug was overtaking my thinking, or I was too nieve to know. All teenagers usually experiment with either drugs or alcohol. If they don't it's, I out of 100. If a teenager is too afraid because of what their parents would think or do. If you can't talk to your parents about it,it's most likely not good for you to get into. I know some people try to say it's common sense not to do certain things. I feel that most teenagers run on curiosity. they are very curious as to how things work, or how something is done. They don't have the mentality of leave it alone, again I out of 100.

It kills me that people assume that if an individual is dealing dope that they have a lot of money. They can mistakenly see the person in a car and try to take them out or try to rob them because they assume they have money. I have known some guys that are so busy still buying things because they have dope money that they are still poor and broke. They claim that they are stacking their money but the reality is that they have to live. Some of them have kids too, so I know that they don't have a lot of money. Don't get me wrong their are some who may make a lot of money in one say then someone may make in a lifetime, but this is fast money and fast money is not good money.

There are some people who have attained a life of stardom. They and the people in thier family seem as to have money. That all depends on how they manage their money. Most of the stuff that they wear,they rent it. The jewelry they wear they rent it. The cars that they drive they rent them. There is one company as a matter of fact that most of the stars use for renting cars. They are living a normal life that they have worked very hard to have. It is a very hard,hectic, and time consuming life. That's why some of the rappers say how can I kick it or live with a woman or anyone who wants half of my money. I know people who are living poor,middle class, and rich that say that.

There are some teenagers that will do anything for a relationship. I mean they will go to he double hockey sticks and back, for a person that they think they love. There are some teenagers that would rather hang out side of class and mess around with their girlfriend or boyfriend. They would drop all their grades and what ever else concentrating on the person that they like.

There are some teenagers that don't even know how to stay quiet on class. The longest they can stay quiet is three minutes,then it escalates to a loud sound. They mostly talk about what's going on at home. They talk about who's cupcaking with who, I believe that's what we used to call talking to. They are teasing each other about sexually explicit things. I believe that they hope the teacher isn't listening. Again it all goes back to them not being able to whisper either. They can be very cruel to each other also. They talk about beating each other up,then eventually that actually start fighting right there in class. Don't get me wrong, they are warned, sent to dention, or get a call home. These teenagers now tell the teachers to go ahead and call their parents. The result is usually the teacher tells the truth and the student doesn't. If the teacher says that their are problems more than once something is going on with the child. I have seen children lie in their parents face about them not doing anything in the class or towards the teacher. It's amazing what happens after each incident.

There are some grown ups that have adult pressure just like teenagers have peer pressure. I have been a victim of this for a long time now and decided to tell my point of view about it. I go out to a club and I don't want to drink, all my friends act like there's something wrong with me. If I was to drink too much then they would talk about me being wild or loose. I know a guy that never drank before and now he is drinking in the club. It amazed me that people actually smoked weed when they went out. I could not beilieve it, that no one worries about the consequences that come from that. I found out that marijuana will eventually cause insanity, and cause people to think of killing. Marijuana used to be legal and was part of the cause of the great depression. We are now at the point where they are trying to make the poor,thepoor, and the rich,the rich. We must work on ourselves in order to make it in this world. I saw a movie once that gave people their youth back, but the woman said for them to be careful of their bodies. That's life in general,I'm not trying to be Ms. goodie too shoes here, I'm speaking to you.

There are some teenagers who have the opportunity to have another language. To me this is wonderful. I have taken spanish for eight years. My boys get mad at me because they think that, I only speak spanish around latino people. I speak it around them to let them know that we know the language too. I speak it around them to be courteous at times. I also speak it around them to show that all blacks are not illiterate. I let some of the teenagers in school know that I know they are cursing. Latino people are very predjudice against black people. I think it is due to whomever they may have come in contact with. The latino people that I have spoken to, or speak to frequently don't mind me at all. Our teenagers are smarter than grown ups as far as not being predjudice towards each other.   I also think it has to do with ignorant people saying that they should go back to where they came from. From all the people I have talked to there are lots of different nationalities. There are mexican,latino,nicuraguan,bermize,puerto rican, and more. They also don't all come from Mexico and if you talk to them they can tell you. Most people are also predjudice towards each other because of what they hear people say about their culture. Stereotypes are the poisins of the world. People really believe most of the ones that they hear.

As Black people, to me, we don't have a culture. Let me explain, we know that we eat certain foods. We know that are roots come from Africa, but because of slavery all we know is being american. In Africa they have different tribes that have different traditions. Here in the United States we have different holidays that we acknowledge. We only get into different activities due to religion. Not only that we have different ways that we feel regarding religion too. We have a wonderful culture of different people, and people need to get to know that. I know myself that when you are christian you are not supposed to go out to dance in clubs at night. You are not supposed to engage in unwedded sex. There are a whole lot of things. There are the ten commandments,"Exodus20:2-10:And GOD spake all these words saying, I am the Lord thy GOD, which have brought thee out of the land of Egypt, out of the house of bondage. Thou shalt have no other GODs before me. Thou shall not make unto thee any graven image, or any likeness of anything that is in heaven alone, or that is in the earth beneath, or that is in the water under the earth; Thou shalt not bow down thyself to them, nor serve them: for I the Lord thy GOD am a jealous GOD, visiting the iniquity of the fathers upon the children unto the third and fourth generation of them that hate me; And showing mercy unto thousands of them that love me, and keep my commandments. Thou shalt not take the name of the Lord thy GOD in vain; for the Lord will not hold him guiltless that taketh his name in vain. Remember the Sabbath day, to keep it holy. Six days shalt thou labour, and do all thy work. But the seventh day is the sabbath of the Lord thy GOD: in it thou shalt not do any work, thou, nor thy son, nor thy daughter, thy manservant, nor thy maid servant, nor thy cattle, nor thy stranger that is within thy gates."

We know that we were born here in the United States and have to work hard to get where we have to go. We consist of the same three classes as everyone else. There are poor, middle class, and rich black people. The only thing is we spend too much time, talking about and degrading each other on the way we are. There are thugs, bourgeoisie(boozhie), wanna be white,wanna be too black(pro-black), african embraced american,crackheads, dope fiends, wanna be hards, and wanna be softs.

I have got to speak on this seriously, the words spare the rod and spoil the child go in and out of my mind every single day. The government has said that we cannot spank our children. The children have figured out that they can call the police to get their parents in trouble. I know as a black culture,and I have talkekd to a bunch of adults, they say whoop your child. They say that spanking is the best thing you can do for the child. If you are not going to do that then take away what they want the most. For one I know that their are teenagers who will then run from out the house, they will use their friends cell phones, they will go to their friends house and lie about what their going through. The kids try to say that it's because of what they see their parents do. They say that the parents don't do what their supposed to sso they don'l should not have given them lots of money for lunch. I should not have given them a whole lot of things on their birthdays. I should not have given them a whole lot of things through the years. The reason I say this is only because they have become too spoiled. The teens get to where they turn on you. I know that people say that is just teens but it is very hard to deal with. I also told them that if I was the happy homemaker,and a working single mom, they would still have treated me the same way. I was told by a police officer that you can spank your child. To me it's when you try to burn cigarettes, or bruise them to death, or anything else harsh that they are trying to get rid of. To me it is mostly boys that deal with learning things the hard way. People say that it's girls too.

The hardest thing in the world for me to deal with as a single mother is young parents. The teens don't know what they are doing by having sex too early anyway. Does any teen know that they can go to jail for having sex at a young age? If you ask any if they care I'm sure they would say so. I just say two kids about thirteen years old tongue kissing at school and had to tell thme to go to class. I was so upset I couldn't see straight. I have heard plenty of stories of how teens get caught having sex at school.

They are always disciplined, like suspended or what ever. I have seen young girls talking to security gaurds. I see them talking to male teeachers or administrators. I know that's what we say, all the teens hormones are jumping off, but it scares me at times. It makes me wonder where did they get their experience from. Some people say that most girls are just like that. I know most boys are copying off of single fathers that are trying to teach them how to treat girls. I remember a boy that use to see his brother with a girl having intercourse, while heis mother was gone. Being a young parent is hard because you need to raise a person. Their are diapers,food, and clothing to provide. After that it is education that you must provide for them. Elementary school always is just half a day, and if you haven't gone to college, you will have to work and go to college when you get older. Always remember when you have a baby you are having an adult. It is not a joke, and if you don't believe in an abortion, then it is up to you to deal with. I know a young woman who said if she had a baby her mother would take care of it. I know back in the day our parents were like you laid down you have it. To me that shouldn't be the answer, if the children are too young, give it up for adoption, or find a way to not get pregnant too early. You know one person told me, what about abstinence. I have just recently decided on abstinence and I would say it is hrder than trying to find the right man. Guys ask me am I gay, they ask me why not me(like I sleep with every tom, dick, and harry), they ask me over and over to be with them in bed. I know for most teenage girls they are looking for a father figure, and for the boys they are looking for a mom. The problem is this goes on into adulthood and still sticks to the heart.

I would like to talk about another touchy subject,teens stealing. There is a lot of loss behind teens stealing the things that they want. For one with money, when you steal from your parents you are taking money from the house, bills, and car. They may not care, but if they were to go to jail or juvenile hall they would care. Some teens may say that it's a way to survive because their parents are poor. I know some parents who always cry poor but a lot is spent on movies, dvd's, gadgets for the home, and a whole lot of other things. As far as a store goes, the store looses money if the person is caught or not. Then the store still has to make up the money that was lost so they hike up the prices. I know teens that tell their parents I want to steal when I go to the mall. I say don't go to the mall then. I also say that through voting their is a way to still get in trouble for stealing. If a child doesn't get caught it's not good because then they go on to bigger and better things. In reality it is not better, it hurts their character and their parents character. Their are actually some black people who own businesses and in that case you are stealing from your own people instead of helping them to come up.

I have been around teachers and have heard stories of a teacher being attacked by knife point. I have heard of teachers getting robbed. I have heard stories of teachers getting things thrown at them. The teachers are human beings, they don't get paid half of what other careers get paid. They have a lot to do in a day whether it is disciplining unruly kids. They have to be psychologists,mothers,fathers,confidants(friends in secret), chef, and a whole bunch of other titles. Some of them feel that the students are children and they are only their to teach. Some teachers may like you or not like you, but you still need to get an education. Most teachers have the privilege to change schools if they want to. Most kids would say so, but you are missing out on a great education that you will definitely need later. Most teachers that I know have had corporate jobs, have degrees (bachelors, masters , or doctorate). There are some teachers who have been scientists, and the years that they have taught is amazing. Now teens always think someone is old when their in their thirties. I feel your not old until you die. Most people say your only as young as you feel. Some teachers have 20,30,40,50 years on thier belt of working plus teaching for 20 or 30 years. People don't retire until their 65 years old and their thinking of raising that to 69. I don't see how teachers have gone as far as they have. Most people know that if it weren't for teachers we wouldn't have star atheletes,actors, actresses, chefs, directors, singers, musicians, and a whole bunch of other careers.

The thing that amazes me the most is that teens to me look like they are really admiring stars and the money that they have. Most of the jewelry and clothes that they wear are borrowed for the night,weekend, or whatever. There are some stars who have a lot of money that actually live with millions of dollars. I know that it all isn't a picnic. You see on the shows, how they are hounded by the media. They have to pay bills too. They have to deal with possibly getting robbed, their kids being taken, sending their kids the right way into this great world of ours. They have to deal with relationships, whether they are bad or good. The stars have to deal with the same things that poor, middle class, and rich people do. The only difference is that they have more money to deal with. They also have more cars,houses,employees, or just maintenance for themselves to pay for. I would wish that the teens would admire them from afar, and either plan to grow up and go to college to be like them, or just watch them on tv and be an individual.

I hear all over the place from teens how they want to drive. A car is one of the most deadliest weapons on earth and if you don't learn to drive properly it is hard to do. Their is drivers ed, but there is also driving school. Just going tdown to the dmv and taking the test is not the only two things to driving. All teens need insurance. If you don't have it you can have your car taken away. Insurance however is higher for teens because they don't use good judgement when driving. They are more risky by smoking marijuana(weed), and drinking while driving. They just don't think that doing certain things like cutting people off, or going over the lines, or hanging out of the car is something stupid. I was told that a girl was hanging out of the roof of a van when the van got hit and she went flying and died. The teens didn't want to tell that part, anything that you can't tell your mom,can't be good for you. There have been plenty of accidents behind drunk driving, and there are deep consequences for that like life without parole. A teen can be put in adult jail now if they shoot somone, so think about driving,seriously. I have heard of countless stories of how teens have gotten road rage and just shot somone behind it. I know for certain that a guy tried to run me off the road and I went behind him trying to intimidate him after he got mad because I wasn't going fast enough, but I had to think no we could get into a serious confrontation. I became the adult and went on to where I was headed. Road rage can come into a lot of diferent things, getting mad at a teen who is taking their time across the street. The person in the car is supposed to give the right of way, but that doesn't give the teen the right to go slow as molasses across the street. It's like their saying oh you ain't gonna hit me, when the person in the car may have kids and needs to get to work on time before money is taken out of their check. The adult may be in the hurry to the hospital. When someone yells curse words at you because they are mad because your turning to slow, you may not know where your going. Think about being responsible while driving.

I knew that inflation was coming, and it has happened before in my life, but it really finally hit me this time. I was so impacted by the prices raising on everything,gas, food, etcetera(etc.). I used to tease the boys about mcd's being 10 dollars a piece when they grew up. All of the fast food restaurants have gone up to five dollars a meal. If you think about it, even with the dollar menu, you spend more , than what you would spend for a meal, if you don't watch out. The gas prices going up to 2 dollars and some change per gallon, is hard to deal with. I can only get two gallons now with five dollars. Black people probably ain't spending two dollars no more, if they do they won't get far. It takes 20 dollars, or a little more to fill up my tank now. I have always ate the cheapest costing bread in the store. I know some people who only eat one kind of bread and still buy it. You can learn from people where to go to get the right prices for food. My mom has only always dealt with the sales in the wednesday or sunday newspapers. I thought I was poor before but man.

Going to college as an adult is harder. I waited thirteen years to go to college. I didn't think that college was the answer. I wanted to try to work my way up in the businesses that I worked for and make it that way. I have been working since I was fifteen. I have always had the level of mind that I problem of going in circles, or having to quit do to not having the maturity level of mind that I have now. That is thanks to college, and friends that support me and try to tell me about different jobs. The reason I thought about college is because I had two boys and I wanted a better life for them. I struggled through getting a bachelors at CSUHayward. I rushed into that because a substitute teacher told me that I didn't have to have an associate degree to get a bachelors degree. It was so hard working,going to college at night, and taking care of two boys, while staying with my mom. People have called me crazy in the first place to work with children at school, and having two of my own. Plenty of people have said that they couldn't do it. The best thing besides the education that I learned from college is networking. I talked to so many people before I went to college, then I learned that that is another way of learning information, and getting to know more people. I met a guy who said that he worked in movies and that it was his college buddies that would tell him about the casting calls. I obtained a loan while in college so I am thirty thousand dollars or more in debt. If I find the right job then I can get rid of it. If it weren't for college I would not be writing. Last year I had four jobs to pay for the last book I wrote. This year I only have two jobs,and attend two colleges,Laney, and Film Arts Foundation. I have always had big dreams and I put them on the back burner from time to time. I have to keep pushing on for myself ,my two boys, and my mom.

When I first heard the words no child left behind, I thought it meant that the school districts would not keep back the children that couldn't make it in school, from graduating. i was thinking ok, then why are they tesing the children to see if they could hang in the first place.I saw on tv a conference on the special ed children not being left behind. I have been with the district for a very long time and we used to have 7 hours. They cut one hour last year, to save money. Either that ,or they felt that people didn't need the hour. We used to use that hour to have the children catch up on their homework. We used to use that hour to catch up on all the classwork they may not have been able to finish. Each child is on a different level just like regular students. It may take the child a long time to do one thing and a short time to do something else. There are some students in special ed who become independent and can obtain 4.0 grade averages. As far as testing the regular students, this is hard on them also. They may not have grasped the classes they were supposed to,therefore they won't pass the test. They may not have grasped the concept of reading,believe it or not, even by middle school. So by the time they get to high school somehow they have gotten by, or learned to adapt. Those children are the ones that are the most unruly(out of hand), the ones that the teacher has to calm down. Now of days that could be the whole class. I remember my seventh grade teacher not being able to teach because the whole class was acting up. I see the same thing happening now. When the parents or anyone of high stature comes in they are calm. Sometimes it depends on the parent whether they will get tremendously out of hand or not. They do have discipline in progress at the schools. If this is all teenagers than it it going to continue to happen. It's like their trying to rebel but they don't know how. Their rebelling to stop learning, back in slavery days peole black people werkilled,mamed,decapitated, or whatever else if they tried to learn. I heard kids say that school feels like prison. School is no caomparison to prison,except being held in one place, for six hours. In prison you can get held from over night, to the rest of your life,that's different.

I would love to get a politician to come to the school for at least a whole month, and deal with the kids in Oakland. I know then that it would be different. they would probably have body guards everywhere they went. There would be so much publicity they may not even be able to teach. It would only last for a little bit and then school would go right back to normal. I understand that the schoold districts have a budget, but cutting peoples' jobs who need them, and can't go to anything else, is not fair. I always tell the caucasian teachers that they have no problem with going to another school district. If a black teacher tried, they may be the token one,OOPS! We no longer have affirmative action. I'm sure politicians would not retire and become teachers to give back to the community. Most people who are caucasian and any other color,latino,asian do not become teachers as a career if they can do better. Some people say that a teaching degree is nothing. I know for a fact that a teaching degree has a part of everyone elses degree. So, how does that not make us smart. I was going to school dealing with teenagers, and my mom. I must have some smarts in there somewhere.

The declaration of independence is currently in the schools. It's in middle school. I see now why grown ups lose their ability to remember what they learned in school. I wish they would put the pledge of alliegance back in school. I was at an elementary school and their was only one teacher that still had the students to say it. I remember in second grade saying it, and being class president for a day. I am still waiting for the first woman president. I hoped it would be Oprah, but most black people end up getting shot when they try to do that. Collin didn't want to do it. I know whoever does better wear a bullet proof vest. I know people say that things have changed but in certain ways they haven't. We as black people still occupy most of the positions in a job that is lower than other people. We are still looked upon as being lazy no good people. As long as we are smiling and being polite. We still have to run from the police. Yes, it depends on if you are drinking,smoking, or doing drugs. Some of it is from just assuming that all black people are alike. In someways we are similar. In some ways we are nothing like each other. There are some black people who hate being black, and there are come who love being black. There are some black people who look down on others. There are some people who will not associate with there own people, and they are black. I was told there are some businesses that are black owned, and have caucasian people to work in them.

What I see now, the things, I see and learn are amazing. I pay more attention now to the things my mom was saying to me as a teenager. She tried to tell me things about Oprahs' shows,the one book from the guy on the signs of men who are no good. He was from sex and the city. I didn't know what she was talking about at first until I saw the show. I told her well I'll be happy when she puts my book on her show. I know that the only way you can get on Oprahs' show being black you have to be famous. I admired Oprah for a very long time, but after a while I used to wonder why she didn't help black people. Then I figured that black people needed to much so that may be why. I thought maybe if I got the chance to ask her I would find out why. I know she helps the children of Africa and that is fine, but there are black people right here in the United States that need help. It would hurt me to here teens say that they didn't like Oprah and I would ask why, and they would say because she does't help black people. Don't get me wrong, Oprah, Whoopi Goldberg (especially because she has dyslexia too), Halle, Janet, and a whole lot of other black women, Mary McCloud Bethune, have always been my role models. I also think the children get confused by tv not being real and the people not being real because they don't get to see them in person. If it was up to me I would want to get a program where stars could come and talk or perform for the kids at middle and high school. I also believe in what Bill said, i know now that if you want to improve yourself you must go to college to learn more. I know some people have other obligations but you need to make a way to go. I know as a people we would have a lot more by having more marriages that are good and sound, owning our own businesses, and helping each other as a community to learn how to do the different things that we need. I think Dubois and Marshall had the right idea, but because of modern times, you need to go to college and work to provide for yourself.

I always tell children to be a child while you can. You don't have long to do this, and you need to plan to have your life in order so that you can work towards being whatever you want to be. I have told people all my life that I wanted to be like Oprah. I had one guy just recently who said you can be like Oprah. That is just pushing me more, to get my goals together and to keep writing just to see what happens. When teens try to find themselves they want to do what the grownups do, by staying out late. They want to experiment with drugs like their parents. My pastor just said in church today, that the children are following the adults examples. I told my boys that as adults we have earned the right to go out,drink,smoke, or whatever we want to do. We must do it within reason because of the The law, but we are adults now. I know part of the problem is young parenting. I had the boys in my early twenties, older then some but still too young. I didn't want there to be a generation gap between them like myself and my mom. She had me in her early thirties, you also have to be careful of having children too late. By the time your older you will be to old to handle the teen age problems. Teenagers trying to fight back, and trying to assert themselves. You never know how much training an adult has had, and if you push them too far you never know what they can do. These children need to learn to respect adults. If it's just me let me know, but too many of the teens now are talking to adults any kind of way. They are very disrespectful to woman, like they want to seriously hurt them. When they grow up what do you think they will become. That's why it's better for it to be two parents, so that the child can have a balance in there life. If the father is an abuser it makes the boys turn into abusers also, and the men act like they don't care or they don't know. If you didn't want it done to your mom, than don't do it to other women. There are a lot of men who are against this, they don't like the fact that men beat woman, and they tell the women to beat the men. I know it has to do with poverty,love,and just sympathy. It also has to do with protection,and not wanting to be lonely. It also has to do with finding a father or mother figure.

There are a lot of teens that have cell phones now. The price per month for a family of three can be more than 150 dollars. The phones alone cost to buy. Then we pay for the monthly bills to use the phone. It is so crazy. Everytime I think about paying the bill I want to cut them off. The children get the phones taken away ususally, if they are seen using one. You just don't know if they are talking to a friend or not. My boys will argue that most of the time it is me calling them to pick them up ,or to find out where they are going after school. The teens only talk to each other about school,parents, or their relationships. The boys get happy off of how many girls numbers they have. The girls get happy off of the boys calling them. There are some teens who have mutual friends. In that way I think the tenns are better at it than some grownups. I watched a student sneak to get on the phone, then the student got caught by the teacher and the phone was taken away. I know about a student who tried to get a phone back from a teacher herself, then later the mother came in to get it. Most of these children have attitudes behind taking away the phone.

Why is it that at even thirteen through sixteen teens still whine. They love to whine about what they don't have. They love to whine about not having any food in the home(not what they want to eat). They love to whine about doing chores around the house, and act like they do to many already. I always tell my boys that I used to have to wash the walls. I had to wash the dishes. I had to vacuum the floor. I had to wash and fold my and my mothers clothes. I had to turn around after that and clean up my room. All the whinning that they do usually gets on my nerves. To me I think that they are looking at what their friends have and they want to have it. From what the kids tell me they just want something that they see and they want it. Then they see all the outfits on tv from the singers, rappers, and actors and actresses. They want to impress each other when they are teens. Then when you become adults they say that women only notice what women are wearing. Women only notice the bad guys, or the good looking guys. We've got a crazy mixed up world when it comes to clothes,especially the drooping pants, and just like back in the day the teens today say, it's only a style. My boys both say why can't teens just dress the way they want to dress, and it will be allright they don't see how stereotypical it looks with some droopy(saggin' jeans), a hoodie(sweatshirt with a hood), and those tall tee shirts to cover their behind. My mom didn't understand the bright colors I used to wear.

I read in the paper yesterday that their were 88 homicides last year. there were some people who were shot to death and their ages were between 17 and 35. That is a really sad number,let alone some of the ones that may have not been solved yet. It makesd me think about all the people that have passed away in my life, and in the past few years. My grandmother passed away in two thousand, her brother, and her sister the year after that. My cousin in Kansas city, My grandmothers friend,My babysitter, the guy down the street and the guy around the corner. There have been three people from karaoke that have passed away. It is all so sad. It is also because of them that I wanted to get myself together before it was too late. A life is a beautiful thing, you have a lot of ups and downs, but you still need to strive to work hard and survive.

Nobody's Perfect, I want all teens to know that all adults are not perfect. The teens look up to us, as the most highest being they have ever known besides GOD. I am so upset that they feel that we are to get everything right. They feel we have to say everyhting right. They feel that what we teach them has to be right also. I here from my boys, to the teens in school, that what I say is wrong. One teen I know laughs at me even when I'm typing on the computer, typing the wrong letters. I know that thye don't know any better. I know that they are still trying to find themselves, but it's hard. No one to me is perfect, but GOD. To people who believe in their own infinite spirit, or people who are atheist still know that no one is perfect.

I have learned over the years that their are only certain black people that speak using proper english. I know that our language was different coming from slavery and Africa. I know that most of us are american so therefore most black people don't know anything but english. There are some black people that you can't even understand. There are some teens that you cvan't understand because all they speak is slang. Every teen generation tries to make up thier own language. When we were young there were things that we used to say like tight,what's up,cool(which is still my favorite),you see what I'm sayin'. Now they have other words that the teens use. They don't care if they matter to adults or not, but the words mean a lot to them, because they have a language that adults don't understand.

Every since I was younger because my mom taught me proper english, every one said that I was trying to be white. You might want to use it sometimes because your not going to get anywhere in this world without it. You know,people got mad because Bill Cosby said that more black people should go to college. He at least may have said that if they want to get some where they need an education. I tried to tell a man, we had a great conversation, about how I feel about the subject. He said that he didn't have time to go to college. He said that he had to take care of his wife and his baby. I told him that no matter when he got the chance to go to college. I waisted thirteen years, until I went. I am currently going to two colleges at the same time. I still have times when I am flat broke, but I wouldn't change it for the world. I asked GOD to help me pull through, and many of times he has created miracles. I know now that school is the answer. I say to all black people don't get mad at the man, when the man is in college. I have talked to many caucasian people and they say that they have gone to college. Some of them have jobs, or their own businesses, and are still taking classes. I know that college helps you to learn how to network. College overall teaches you, believe it or not, to think more than you ever have before. The reason I say that is because I know a lot more now than I did before because of going to college. I know now that anything you want to know about business, psychology, anything you can think of, is in college.

I always tell my boys that the only I really have to buy is one pair of shoes, one pair of pants, one shirt, and one jacket if needed. I have spoiled them so much over the years I hope their is definitely a good future for them. I have bought things for them all year long so when christmas came, they didn't need anything. I know now alot of the teens have the name brand clothes. They have those high priced 200 dollar shoes. Their clothes end up coming to a total of 3 to 400 dollars at the store for the next few months. We parents spend so much time now, trying to give our kids what we didn't have, that they may not appreciate it. I know with my own and some teens that I see, they act like your supposed to give them a lot. Then they come up with all the stories about I don't have this or that , and I need it. Really it is a want, not a need. If your sitting there with ten pairs of jeans, and a stack of shirts, and four to five pairs of shoes, you are doing darn good. When the teens get the chance to buy their own things, then they'll start to appreciate it. The other thing is the other teens teasing the children about what they wear. That makes me so mad. I tell my boys If, the child that said it can't buy you something else, than everythings allright. I also tell the teens I know that their parents had to buy what they have on, so stop being mean. Teens can be so cruel to each other though.

I am so outrage with the teens that think they know it all. As a parent I taught my boys since before pre-school. I have gone to school myself, have a bachelors, and I'm still going to school. Because I am grown and the way my mom taught me, I don't feel that I know it all. These teens now think that they know it all because they know more information than their parent may know. They are currently in school and that is great that they are learning information. They can tell you some info backwards and forwards. They can tell you some details, a little about some things, and some things they may not know a lot about. It all comes down to learning something new. People have to update their education. There are lots of things that we parents know, thanks to our education. I know now that when there is something you need to know, just look in a college catalog. I often went in cirlces for years trying to figure out what to do for my future. I even got scared after going back to college again, not wanting to go. I'm glad I did, and I'm happy now, that I went to class all over again. You can sit,sit,sit,sit,sit, but if you don't get off your butt and do something you will stay stuck in the present, and the present will become the past.

It's so important for the teens to have them to help with the grandparents. When they do that it helps them to understand what their grandparents are going through. I know with my granny it was hard dealing with her in her last days. I know seeing Jamie Fox cry behind his grandmother, is so cool. I know that I am doing all this because of my mom and my granny, along with my boys. We had hard times, very hard times, and some great times with granny. I know with my mom she takes five hours in the store. Like she says we can't eat if we don't help. I try to ask my mom ab out my granny and her mom before her. I feel if we had more of a lineage,black people would be together better. Our ancestors are important, our great-great grans, and people before that are important. The parents and grandparents are dying, and we need to have a heritage. Some people have lost their grandparents together, or one behind the other. To me the black families were broken at slavery, then the books were burned so that we could not remember what happened. No matter what happens we are always effected by slavery. Back in slavery days they used to say the only way to keep a black person from knowing anything,put it in a book. Here it is yall,read it and use it the best way you can.

I don't know now if teens are doing things for other people to be nice, or to get something in return. They want to get allowance and they want you to just hand money to them. I tried to do the allowance thing, it worked out good at first. Then when I got to where I couldn't pay anymore, my teens got the nerve to act like they were taking it out on me. Their grades started going down in school. I have struggled for so long with that, I am tired of trying. I will still keep pushing them but I don't have tto much farther to go. They will be 21 years of age after a while and I will be free from fussing every morning, afternoon, and evening. Somtimes teens need to do something for someone just because it was a nice thing to do. You don't have to be nice,just to get something in return.

I feel there are some teens that don't realize their responsibilities. I have taught my teens to cook,wash clothes, and clean the house. But I always tell them about how I used to clean the walls. I tell them how I used to have to vacuum each room in the house. I tell them how we used to hang the curtains. I know that when they were little,washing clothes was no joke, because I was washing for three people. I admire the women who come home after work, no matter what they do, and cook,clean,or whatever else. There are 365 days a year,lets not count the weeks, and we are normally trying to figure out what needs to be done. The main reason we are trying to teach you how to do the work, is so that you can take care of yourself. Some teens say taht we are trying to treat them like a slave. They don't think that we are being treated like slaves too. We have to go to work everyday,we have to stay at the same job, and if you don't have education then what.

Some people may say that you don't have to have an education to make it in life. I know for the simple fact that when I was at my old jobs, I never moved up any higher, without an education. Some people are happy with the amount of money that they make. Some people are happy with owning their own business too and those people say that they have been to college. If a person is on a job for thirty years as long as they save money they can be ok. I know someone that was on the job for years and they went to school because I kept talking about it, they moved up to a supervising position. I have tried to tell a lot of people to go on back to school, or to school for the first time. I feel if I can do it than anybody can. I have tried and struggled so hard to have a better life for myself,boys, and mom.

I know there are some teens that have to see something in order for it to be real. I can't describe it, it's like they feel nothing is going to happen to them. I told my teens that if they decided to deal dope that there would be someone pimping them. The dope game goes a very long way, and it is sad to see all the black people that are getting murdered because of it. I know that people say you gotta hold your own, but I wish that the dealers could be taught to read or whatever they need to get what ever they want. I'm not saying that dope dealers are dumb at all. I know and went to school with a few of them and they had A grade point averages. I don't meant to ruin their rep but it's true. I grew up with some of the coolest ones, and they admired my friend and I because we worked and weren't sitting at home doing nothing. I know there are some dealers where there may have been some teachers they may have thought that they were just the worst people in the world but it depends on the individual. We are killing our own, but what if black people became extinct. I saw in a history story that marijuana made people insane, and mostly other cultures were selling it. I know that a lot of different things are being sold now, and you have to think about why it's being pushed. They don't care if you get rich from it because sooner or later black's will kill other black's,innocent women and children. It's like Iraq, it's a war in the united states. You can best believe to that if it came down to black against white, who will get the president(democrat or republican) to push the button.

I have been reading through the study bible. There are some deep stories in there. It is the niv version,and the other information that I wrote is from the king james version of the bible. This bible talks about meaningless things that we take for granted. It tells the truth about wanting wealth. It says that GOD will give it to you but if you get to greedy them someone else will take it away from you. Also everyone says that if you use it for his good,he will give it to you too. The book talks about someone being like the boss,and there will always be someone higher than them. It talks about generations to come, one after the other and it is meaningless. It talks about war and what the outcomes are, of course the ones who come out of top are the ones who believe in GOD. People have always complained about GOD being a jealous GOD. They say that they don't like that part. I think it means that people can have their different religions,but make sure that you put him first. We do that, I don't care what kind of religion their is we all believe in one higher being or spirit and that is GOD. It talks about knowledge and wisdom. It says what I have always said in life. You can have wisdom, but don't be a fool. That can work both ways, you can be so smart and try to get away with the wrong things, or you can be smart and do good things. Everything is in the bible just read it, sooner or later I am going to read the whole thing. I remember when I was younger, I used to question church and the bible. I remember when I didn't know anything I would ask a deacon or the pastor. Now I am of christian faith still, but not baptist. I love my church. You know, every religion has it's predjudices' too. I wish that all the religions' would get together and say ok enough is enough and fix the world. It says in the book that people used to follow rules of GOD. It says how to cook the food. It says how to save themselves, for example on the first born story. GOD tells the people where to put the blood and how to cook the animal after. I'm sure they had vegetarians back in that day too. It is all repeating itself, the world is going over again and again. Let's think hypothetically of course, what if the war was about getting rid of some americans and iraqis'. There are too many people in the world. The only way that they can't slim down the earth is too for one get rid of a few hundred thousand, and to pay to explore other planets. But,guess what, there will still be other nationalities eventually there too. Even if the world is destroyed GOD will start over again with each nationality. Think about it,back in the day we used to only have mostly caucasian people on the tv screen. There of course were other nationalities in the world. They just found chinese or some nationality of bones that they say came from the bible days. Another thing that gets my hide. I do not believe in the darwin theory, If we our any other nationality evolved from monkeys, then why aren't they changing in front of our eyes now. Come on think about it,if you put a man next to a monkey for x amount of year, the only thing that will happen is one of 'em will die first. Man don't get me started. The only reason we don't have a black president is because for one someone may get shot, and for two we don't want to deal with all the stress that a president goes through. The only reason are kids are bored in school maybe because their all geniuses and we can't do enough for them, to learn, all they want to know. I haved come to find though that black kids do a lot better when it comes to touching and feeling. When it comes to lab,art(music), listening(can work as long as it's not boring), and sports.

I come to think that if we could let the students stand for five minutes while writing the do now may change thins, just to give them something different to do. Maybe with one arm behind their back they can write spelling words five times each. Maybe have a spelling bee, but after the word is spelled right they can do five jumping jacks. To me the teens have become so bored with work that all they want to do is have some fun while doing it. I know that's not reality and the world doesn't always work that way. Because of the way tv has changed and the movies, they are getting into a more hyper state. To me because of the imbalance they feel that the world is not right so I'm going to do wrong to. Which adult out there has not don't something they weren't supposed to when they were a teen. I not saying that they have to make the wrong choices I am just saying that here is our future. I'm sure that's how my mom used to feel. I just told her yesterday that I wouldn't want to be elderly now. I know how much crime and whatever else is going on, and I don't like it. I am not going to be trapped in my house behins it though. think about it back in the day the slaves used to have to hide out,stay on the porch, or just plain stay to themselves. We as a people do not need to go back to that, why can't we just all be intellegent (yes as intellegent as or maybe more than the white folks) and just get done what we need to.

Another thing I get very upset from is that people say that we shouldn't be mixin gospel with rnd b and things like that. I feel we as a black people should embrace whatever a black person is doing. My coworker and I always fuss over it because she says that if an artist is a gospel artist and then switches to r and b that's not right. But then I aksed her if an artist goes from r and b to gospel then that's right. She said yes, that the person shoould stick to what their doing. She said that people arent's supposed to be singing gospel and then later droppin it like it's hot. I say that either way it's going to be done anyway. Back in the day we took the artists no matter what because we were fighting as a people to get Black people out there. I mean look at all the past artists their are all kinds from the past. Their are a lot of different authors,atheletes, and scholars. I say we need to have change. I may get mad at gangster rap but it's still here. Listen closely to Tupac and Biggie.

I know now that Fifty cent and Game and, all the other ones after them, need to stop. For one they are already in an area that not too many people can get to. They are gonna turn around and repeat the same thing as Tupac(toopock), and Biggie. Think about it, another way to get rid of a hell of a lot of people,genocide(jino side), another way to get rid of black people. Come on Black on Black crime, alot of niggas' die. Then innocent people die too, the ones who tell, and the ones' who look like someone else. Come on now we think we all look alike to. I can just here some guys now in the car,fixin to do a drive buy, uhm I thought that nigga' was uhm t' stack. The game is very serious, and our people again ain't even thinking straight. Oh yeah let me tell you about that being macho, your pride gets to you so much don't just get it in your head that it's not right. Tupac said that he had a baby to show some of the innocence that he had in him. Come on think it about it my black people, Tupac was just at the beginning of his game,the true game, and he couldn't change his image. Iced T did it, the arguments got so big between him and Biggie like that,that's not good. Let's say hypothetically speaking that Neither Tupacs boys or Biggies' boys did anything. Let's say it was the man,because people tell rumors so much,it's like the game of telephone, and someone each killed both of them. Let's say that one of the guys were paid by the man to get rid of each one of them. I 'm just saying that it's all not worth it, and then in a way it is. The reason I say that is because if it wasn't for each one of there gifts we wouldn't know the stories of what they used to live like, but we have to change things.

A friend and I discussed crack and ecstasy babies. She was saying that all the babies that are being born now are going to grow and to be crack and ecstasy babies, and that's not good. I know that most of yall know that crack kills, but do you care? Ecstacy is killing our youth. Their have been stories in the papers about young girls taking it and dying. I know some children who were at a party and the guy gave a girl some ecstasy. These teens are living in an adult worold and we as parents need to tell them about things. Back in my day, not that I'm too old, our parents didn't tell us much of the horrible stuff because they wanted to proctect us from it. I know that then when I became grown that I had to live it the hard way and find out for myself. I am not the only teen out of a million from my generation that went through that. Even my mom says that she didn't have to go through all the things that I went through. I feel it is because her day was different than mine, and even now.

Then I know that she has a different mentality than myself. She didn't take no mess and she wasn't going to get into it, even now she keeps to herself mostly and she is ok with that. Don't get me wrong she has a lot of friends, but she is not around them a lot. They know her and she knows them, and if anything was to happen to her their would be hell to pay. I used to think that my mom and grandmother were like the mafia. They would take care of my four girl cousins and myself, and still get things done. My granny used to cook up the behind for christmas and thanksgiving,I miss her.

I know for the simple fact that every caucasian child I talk to they get to travel to Paris,Hawaii,Jamaica,etc. I know with my boys, and a lot of other black teens, and they don't get the chance to travel. I have wanted all my life to travel to Paris, Jamaica,

Italy, Greece ,Mexico,and everywhere else for that matter. I look over my head while I am at work, all the time I dream of being in the air being whisked away to some far off place. I listen to Janet, who I have idolized for years, and try to picture the places that she sings about. Every or mostly every girls dream is to be a dancer and singer like in the videos. I have always wanted to perform on stage just like her. I wanted to be able to change my wardrobe, finish the show, get into my limo and fly to Venice for the next concert. I watched the travel programs for years, from Robin Leech to alot of different shows of how the stars, and the royalty live. People say not to dream so big, I like to think of what

I do as research, so far all I know is Jackie Collins that writes books about the stars. One day I hope I can gain there confidence, just like Gordon Parks did with the people he took photographs of, and can write about them too.

I heard some men talking about their businesses. There are actually very porminent black men out there who have businesses. When I tried to finally ask question, one man told me that it is still hard for black men to get loans for business. I don't think they have companies that say bancruptcy,bad credit, we'll give you loans to start your own business. I know fro myself that it is hard to start your own business, due to the money. Then on top of that if they did give me a loan, I wonder about being able to hold my own so that I can pay the loan back. Is it that men have to save up for years and years to have their own business, plus take care of a wife and children too. To learn the different parts of a business you can go to college to find out how it's done. You must clear up your credit,even bancruptcy only lasts for so long. You have to budget your money so that you can eventually check out your own building, or space. Always,Always, check things out first, so you can have in the future what you have to do. You can plan out how much you will need and how long it will take. That's another thing, I had to learn over the years, but I really always new it. When I was in elementary all the way 'til now, I knew that the only people that had the bmw's,benses,and town cars, were the older,senior adults. I always wondered does it have to take that long. No it does not,

not If you go to college. We might get mad at the man but the man is going to college. There has only been one caucasian man that is rich, or has good money. He said that he didn't ven go to college, and it's not hard what he does. Although from my observation he keeps up his body, he is always well dressed, and he is a people person. He also has two companies, so hey it can be done. But I always say for black people until we can get some kind of mutual leverage here, we need to go to college.

We talked about how the devil is present. I have always felt that way with people killing other people. All the diseases,plagues, or whatever else we've had. We have had SARs, Aids, mad cow disease, killings of three, four, or eight people. Lately the weather has been so crazy as far as being on and off, hot or cold, it's strange. A guy in the barbershop said that it was due to global warming. There are so many random shootings now,it's ridiculous. The crazy thing is that lately one was at a court house and one was in a building where the people were having church service. The black man that shot in the courthouse killed four people total, and the caucasian man in the church killed eight people. The black man surendered at the end with a white t-shirt, and the caucasian man killed himself.

Black people are no longer demanding an education! They mostly feel that they need to get there own businesses or just hustle as they call it. I know for a simple fact that Martin Luther KIng and all the rest of the blacks from the past are probably turning over in their graves. There are people coming from other countries,Afric a,Asis,Mexico to get an education. We,Black people, are here and have been here, and are not taking advantage of education. We as Black people either from defying our parents, or just thinking that we're too smart. We need to open legal businesses,get legal loans, and make something out of Oakland. If things cannot be done like that , then the system has to be changed. I have seen a few places now that are still mostly caucasian in employees. Black people to me don't sue like they do. There have been places of employment that are mostly arabian, or chinese too. A friend of mine said that we as Black people need to have businesses like that too. I guess I'm like a modern day Martin Luther Kingette, I would like us to all have businesses that everyone can work at and not dominated by just one race. We have to look at it in reality too. I know that everyone wants to own family bussinesses only. Most people get a business and then have all their family members work for them. I know that I have taught my boys to not be predjudice, and they have all kind of friends. Their friends and families of their friends have taken good care of my boys while I was at work or at college. I am a people person and speak to anyone and everyone. My son thought that I was predjudice, and I tried to explain to him that there are a lot of differences in this world. Truthfully until black people change things in a positive light, our world will not get better. I also tell them I am just telling them whats real, there are latinos who have a whole block to themselves. There are people with businesses in china town. The arabians have sewn up the liquor stores, and small markets. When will we as black people get our own place in the palace too.

There are still truant officers out there. I was amazed, when I was working at a fast few restaurant just a few years ago, and met a Black woman truant officer. I mentioned to her then that I didn't think they had any offficers in the school district anymore. I know back in the day,not too long ago, we had so many truant officers that teens always went to school. Now people say that truant officers only do something when the child is out for a long time, or if they have committed a crime. I know for a simple fact that you need to control the ones who try to stay home for just a day or too also. For one they miss out on a lot of information, and for two they challenge their parents to try to not go to school. You know,people say you can whip your kids, but when they become teens they are to big. I know that Ihave told my boys that they cannot miss school because they are black. I aslo tell my boys that they are never to big for a whoopen. Then there is also the teens that go to school, but don't spend time in the classroom. They hang all around the school all day, and even some of them run from the teachers or whatver. Their are some that threaten the teacher, or act up in class just so they can get kicked out of class.

The students think that it is cool to act silly in class. The boys may draw dirty pictures on the board, the boys may go into a class of a teacher, and are not supposed to be there. There are students that literally try to scare teachers now. They can say over and over again that the teacher is not scared of them, but the way that it looks is that he is. I know as an adult it would have to be a group on me, to get me to bow down. I don't care what the nationality of person is, you need to see your child in class. The kids thanks to the parents are confusing predjudice with shame, confusion, and it's sad to see everyday. These kids think Matilda, is real. When the parents come they act normal for the day, and then for the next day they act up. They even challenge the teachers now, they think they know more than the teachers. they say that the school is bootsy because of the ways the walls are.   They room may be written on,on every wall. The water fauscets have been spit in, or the roof leaks. All the money the city used to fix up the schools, just wasn't enough.

Currently there are supposed to be thirty students to a teacher. Now that they have all the schools closing there is going to be more chaos. What will there be fifty students to one teacher. I can remember when I was in juior high, the teacher couldn't teach because the students were too rowdy, and loud talking. Are they trying to say that they don't care whether our black teens go to school? Are they trying to say that there is no use in sending them to school, because their going to jail, or growing up into dope dealers anyway. I know that this is not meteor man either, we do not need to be in one area with one dominant people on top,dope dealers, and non-dope dealers on the bottom. Only because their will be too much killing and people will be trapped. Pay attention to the movie with the dope dealer that started the b's and the c's, then tried to tell them that he wasn't right. This is not Blade either. You cannot get rid of the old school because they have a lot of knowledge. Even if you get rid of the young generation, you could be getting rid of the next president that may help us all. Until everyone wake's up, as Spike Lee said back in the day, we won't ever rise.

There are a lot of teen that are not doing their homework. Tests and homework are the main part of the teens grades and they don't want to do it. They claim that all the work is to hard ,and their parents can't help them. The only way that the parents are able to help them is if they can sit in the classroom for about a month maybe even more than that. I gaurantee ypu that if more parents sat with these teens the teens would get a better grip on life. I heard of some parents that beat up on a principal, yeah it may be because she was white, but what is that teaching the kids. I'm sure that they ended up going to jail or whatever but come on people, that's why Martin said to be peaceful. Yeah, he may have gotten shot but we wouldn't be were we are now if it wasn't for them. I know as teens I try to tell them that they wouldn't want their daughter beat up by no group of kids. I know that they wouldn't want their son shot by somebody. Why are we having war right here in the city, instead of saving lives and letting everyone else live their life. Why are we as a people taking from one another, it's like if I don't have it I'll just take it from somone. That makes it worse on someone else the next time.

The teens laugh at the teachers when they play classical music in the classroom. I always tell them that there have been studies that show that classical music makes you smarter. I know to that teachers are trying to replace the music programs that have been taken out of the schools. They also are trying to calm the savage beast, I call it, when they play the music for the teens. I know that even when I get angry I listen to the radio, I listen to kmel, kblx, kissfm, kqed, koit, positive talk radio, and some spanish stations. I decided to play classical music out loud for the hood everybody probably though I was crazy. I

actually like to think of it as a movie sometimes because that is what they use,classical music. When I heard Whitneys' music back in the day I used to say I want music like that when I make it singing. I haven't made it yet, but at karaoke they call me a diva, so I'm happy. My mom taught me to love all kids of music,rock,jazz,co untry,blues,and I learned more thanks to school and tv.

Some teens sit in the classroom and copy off of each other. I know for the simple fact that this is not helping them. When the teens are in elementary school they learn to do work independently(by themselves). It seems that once they get to middle school, they learn how to introduce themselves to friends, and they learn how to copy. Of course, it then turns into the mean, or older kids, asking the teens who always do their work to do it. In high school it gets even worse. The teens are still copying off of each other, or having other teens to do their work. The main reason for the parents to send their teens to school is so that they can learn the information. The teens attend elementary to learn the basic information. Then in middle school they are supposed to gather that information, and keep up their organization skills. Then in high school everything counts as work for college. I guess some of the teens think that nothing is going to come out of going to school. Maybe it's from seeing all the things on television that they see. A lot of people say it's because of the community. Things have got to change!

There are a lot of teens that I see going late to class. They are too busy hanging with their friends, or boyfriend, or girlfriend. The teens don't realize how much of a grown life they are trying to live. I know even in middle school, the teens say if my mom, or dad knew that I had a boyfriend, or girlfriend they would be mad. The adults already know what they want or don't want their teens doing. We already know what it was like in our early age, and teens. When teens go late to class, it is bringing the academic grade down. The teens act like they don't even care if their grade goes down.

Teens have,from what all adults,can see multiple personalities. The children show a lot of anger, regular, or special. They tend to want to destroy property. They curse out the teachers telling them that they are not their parents. They tear up papers, and or books, and they feel that they won't get in trouble for any of it. The teens now a days will act one way with the teacher, then another with the parent in the room. There are some teens who still act the same way even if the parent is right there. They tend to have one way to act with their peers, their mates, and their parents. There is a saying that the irish have,house angel,street devil. A person told me that it can work the opposite way to,house devil,street angel.

Our teens don't have enough black male role models, as teachers. They need to see a male in the room. They also need a black man, because of all the teens that don't have a father figure around. Most people say that a black boy has to have a male of some kind around him so that he can identify with them. The reason they don't have the respect for the women teachers is because of the way the women are treated around them. Plus it is because the olny person that is disciplining them is a woman. They then turn around in the classroom and either try to abuse the teacher, or the other woman that work in an educational setting. It is because of this that it tricles down into their relationships and end up beating and abusing women. This is a deep need for attention! From the whole world, people need to wake up and realize that we will have a lot more killings, or damage to women behind this.

I wanted to say that there are lots of issues going on in the schools with the teens. A lot of the black parents feel that spanking is the answer. They say that since that discipline has been taken away the teens are disrepectful and out of control. There are teens that are undressing in gym right in fron fo the teacher. Instead of just getting dressed in the dressong room, they are waiting to see what sport they are going to play. I know that even in middle school they are not dressing to be cute, or to look good in front of the other students. It is forever cool for the kids to be bad, that it's changing the way society is. It just makes me think what is going to happen to our future. Hopefully the teens will eventually mature into an adult manner and be able to cope in society. I know for the simple fact though that some adults are the same way they were in middle and high school.

Black families are very important, in the fact that, we as people need to improve our culture, and community. The elder's are the most important because they have the most knowledge. They also wer the ones to provide for the next generation. Of course meaning the great-great grandparents, and grandparents. Then then next important are the parents. The next thing are the children. Think of the ancestors from Africa that were brought over. We may not be tied to them now, but even though were american, we need to have some kind of culture. We need to have more black businesses. We need to have more people in higher places,lawyers, doctors, and politicians. I discussed it with a friend, and they said we already have that. They brought up the fact that we need to have our own community seperate from others. Other cultures do it, Latinos, Japanese, Chinese, etc. I know that we have people in higher places but we need more. We are the minority still to this day and nothing feels as if it has changed. People can say what are you talking about, but there has been change, just not enough. Blacks' are still treated as the bottom of the barrel. We are still treated as if we're animals. We are still treated as if we make any kind of noise that we're being too black.

I have been at six different schools. I have volunteered for about two of them, I went to Webster, Frick, and Fremont myself as a child. I have known Oakland's system for a very long time. Now I think of it as giving back to my community. The one thing I want to say of course to the students that are being good in class, wonderful. These are the teens that will have to hold their own when it comes to going to college, and high school! There are a lot of kids that do what they are supposed to do. these are some of the ones that have to deal with the bad ones. We even have a saying that none of the kids are bad. I know for the simple fact that some of them can be really mean and terrible. I know some that act like no one or anything can get to them. I know that the teachers have a way of discipline that they have to follow. I know that the principals have detention, suspension, and kicking the children out of the schools. the only reason a teen has to get kicked out is because everyone has tried everything possible and it will not work. the next step is juvenile hall. Sorry to say this is not the answer. After that the teen is sorry to say doom for the jail house. Most teens shouldn't even want to be in juvenile hall, but I guess they have to prove themselves. Their was a rapper that I heard on late night radio that said the rappers cannot promote being scared of jail because it will make them look like punks. He also said that jail is not one place that he ever wants to go to. Their have been a lot of rappers in life, I am waiting to here from Will Smith again, or LL. They should along with NAS get an award for helping the youth to see a better side of rap. the reason I say better is because the kids need to be in a good light when it comes to living. Right now you should see the way they act because of gangster rap. They say that they are not following behind it, but they can rap it word for word. They are being disrespectful and quoting some of the lyrics from the songs when they say things. Now is their any rapper out there who wants their son or daughter acting like the nard core stuff, or do they want them to be ok. I understand that it's hard for gangsters,dope dealers, and whoever else who may have only one way to make a living, but their is always school no matter how old you get. For them to say theirs only one life for them it's not true. Give back to the community, got to college to learn what you can do to get that homeless person off the street. Go back to college to help get that elderly mom off the streets, who has no one else to turn to. Go back to college just to make you feel like you can accomplish something great. Now don't get me wrong it's not just rap either. It's some r and b songs that these kids listen too that are very harmful. They probably think that they are supposed to go out and do all kinds of weird things to women. They get off on all the skimpy things they wear now. I knew they would soon be wearing string bikinis in videos. I must say all props to snoop with his video with Ferrel where everybody had their clothes on. How many people get mad because of all the black wowmen being exploided in those videos? Let's not talk about all the girls that come to class with the short skirts on and the thongs on. Yes, it is true, there has been a lot of fast dressing over the years of working with teens. A friend told me that one of the rappers said that he may talk about shooting and killing, but he doesn't let his son listen to his music. His son also has a good grade point average. There are other rappers who say that they don't let their children listen to certain music. They also say that when they are out on tour they can still control their children and keep up with them at all times,especially on the phone.

There is a few sheets of information from the Relationship Abuse Prevention Program. The cycle of violence has three things. The first is tension,this is the first phase of the cycle in a violent relationship. The abuser often picks fights and the victim fels like he or she is walking on egg shells. The second phase is violence, some kind of violent attack occurs in this phase, it can be physical, verbal, or sexual assault. the third phase is honeymoon,abuser apologizes for violence, saying it won't happen again. This phase, with no violence can last days,months, or years. The teen power and control states that there are six types of abuse. Threats-making and/or carrying out threats to hurt your partner,threatening to leave,commit suicide, to report your partner to the police,making your partner drop charges or do illegal things. Isolation/exclusion-controlling what your partner does, who they see,talk to, got out with, limiting involvement with friends and family. Using social status-treating your partner like a servant, acting like the master of the castle, making all of the decisions, being the one to define men's and women's roles. Minimize/deny/blame-making light of the abuse and not taking concerns about it seriously, saying the abuse didn't happen, shifting responsibilty for abusive behavior and saying the victim caused it. Intimidation-making your partner afraid by using looks,actions,gestures, smashing things, destroying property,abusing pets, displaying weapons. Peer pressure-threatening to expose your partner's weakness or spread rumors about them, telling lies about your partner to their peer group, manipulating or forcing your partner to do something because everyone else is doing it.

How to fix arguing without violence has six steps. One is to treat all people with respect. Two is tolerate people's differences and try to appreciate them even if they are different from you. Three is not to put other people down. Fourth is to think before you act. Fifth is to take responsibility for your actions. Sixth is to keep your pride in check. There are eight things recommended for understanding equality. They are sexual safety, financial/economic independence, negotiation and fairness, responsible parenting, honesty and accountability, connections with others, trust and suppport, and non-threatening behavior. this information is from the domestic Abuse Intervention Project, Duluth, Minnesota. This was the greatest program I had seen in a long time. I know that the teens are seeing what is going on at home. They would even say what was going on at times at home. It's good that they had someone to ask questions about the issues that are going on today.

Most people always talk about how important it is to buy a home. A person told me that with the first home buyers program you must buy a new home. A friend of mine was shocked to read that a two bedroon home was in the paper for 325,000 dollars. Someone also told me their are some 500,000 dollar homes. I keep telling my boys that by the time they get ready to buy a home they will all cost a million. Now that I think about it there are some out there now. Every ten years the economy changes from inflation. The teens and we adults have to get ready for it. I surprised myself by figuring out that I am not making too much more than I was making ten years ago. Since I have a lot of bills to pay, I still don't make enough money. Besides people always say the more money you make the more bills you have.

Some adults dealt with taking drugs, like smoking marijuana, or snorting cocaine, or dealing with other drugs when they were teens. If they weren't doing them then they knew sombody who was. The teens now a days think that grownups ar too boring, or just don't know what their doing. We used to have all kinds of different types of marijuana back in the day,not to long ago, and other drugs that we had to deal with. Alcohol has been leagal for a very long time. There was a time when it wasn't legal. There was a time when marijuana was legal back in the day. We know all if not most of the side effects that's why we get mad and fuss about a teen doing these crazy things. As soon as a teen gets in trouble behind it, the courts say that they made their own choice,remember that.

There are some restaurants that crack me up when it comes to still serving black people. There are some places who are the greates. There are some places that still go by stereotypes I guess. I went into one place and there were five people in line with two people at the register. It got down to three and one person went to clean the counters. I was in a hurry to get to work so I questioned what was going on. They said that's the way the place works. I went back in there recently and there were seven people in line. There were two people behind the counter, andthree on the other machines. I ask you what is wrong with this picture. I knew when it happened the first time that something was strange. You know the place is great as far as the food and the service, but it makes you think sometimes. I know when I went the next time there probably had been a rush of people,and that's why there were more employees, but. Then there are some restaurants were the service is very fast now. I remember when you had to wait for a long time, if their was a long line of cars. Now there can be a long line or short line and the service is very fast. I saw on the news too, the places with the most dings when it came to not cooking food correctly, or sanitation situations. I know there are a whole lot of people that will still go to fast food restaurants because they love the food.

I have told my boys of the story of Marvin Gaye and his father. Marvin got to out of hand and strung out on drugs and his father shot him. I always try to explain to my teens that a person can get to their breaking point. There are some parents that get like that, sorry to say that's why they end up killing their children. I let them know that these peopl are really,really sick and something is going on with them that they cannot handle. I tell them that it can also happen with some women. You mess with a women too much and something may seriously happen to you. My youngest told me of a rapper that got stabbed by his woman because he was cheating or something like that. the breaking point of a person in general is not good because they either harm themselves, or others. That's why I say no matter what the religion is for the person they need to talk to GOD and see if he can help. Of course their are psychiatrist, or other doctors who can help to. The person needs to talk to someone to help them get out the anger that they have inside. People have a lot to deal with not matter what status of the class level their on. A person can be poor,middle class, or rich, and still have a lot going on. We see so many stories on the news,no matter what's going, about what people are going through. Most people say that we are living in hell on earth.

I want to finish with some other tips also, organization for one. I know from all the schools that I have worked for, or volunteered, and have looked at the children. Most teens have a thing with organization. They have their papers all over the place. They ask the teacher over and over again for another assignment sheet. This is definitely not needed when they just need to look in their binder and find it. Some of the children have the papers not even attached to the binder. They will get the paper from the teacher and throw it in there. All the students are supposed to have dividers for each subject in the binder. With one teacher they are supposed to have dividers for every subject. This may seem like a lot but really it's for the best results for the student. Some of the students just don't care and get rid of the assignments too, then they tell the teacher that they need another one. This takes time away from the class. the student and the teacher may fuss back and forth, the teacher may just be familiar with the student and know that the student is not organized. That's why they ususally tell the parents to go throug the back packs. It's not prying it's keeping the student on track. The other main reason for organization is so you can keep track of your assignments. If you have them in order you know what is done and what is not.

The next tip to talk about is time management. This is the most important because a teacher may give a student up to a month to do something. The next thing you know that month is gone and the assignment is due tomorrow. It's a surprise to the student but not to the teacher because they assigned it. All I can say for this is to write it down in an organizer, binder reminder, or keep a page in your binder just for assignments. In most classes there is a tally sheet. What I do is check off the assignments that have been done, so that I can go back to the ones that haven't been done. It is very,very, hard work to do all this stuff but you've got to do it. Life isn't easy, but you still have to deal with it. I know there are some kids who spend all night, maybe even falling to sleep doing their homework. To those students I give high praise. To the students who may not have the greatest grades, but do all of their work good job. Time management is very important not only in the school system, it will always be very important to when you get a job also. The boss loves an employee that can multitask, and manage all the work in a timely fashion.

When you do get to the age when you can go to work you will need to dress appropriately, and have good hygiene. The first thing a place of employment told me was no wearing your pants half way down your leg. When you go to work you may have to wear a dress shirt, or a cotton shirt that has a collar. Your hair must definitely be presentable. Your jeans, or clothing in general, must be neat. You cannot wear some wholey pants or shoes to the place of employment. The main reson you need to read is so that you can fill out an application with no help. When you go to an interview do not bring a whole bunch of friends with you. The boss wants to see how interested in working,you are. That's also why your parents tell you every night to take a bath. When you go to apply for a job, or for an interview, you should smell your best. Just to give you a side tip, if you smell under the arms while at work, go into the bathroom and wash under your arms,it works! Don't laugh some people from back in the day had to be let go because their odor was offensive. Their have also been some people that I know that have been fired because they dressed the wrong way too. There are rulles at work, just like there are in school. That's why I feel teens should wear unifroms from elementary all the way uup to high school,especially in public schools. Just because it's public doesn't mean that each could shouldn't have to do it.

When you are in an interview you should give the interviewer good eye contact. When you look around and all over the place, then they feel like you aren't confident eonough. I know in a movie back in the day, the guy put his feet on the persons desk during an interview, that is a big no no. You answer the question with a sentence if you can. You let them know that you want the job. You thank them at the end of the interview, and then shake their hand. After the interview is over, a few days later you can send a thankyou card(small one) too.

There also great reasons to keep up your grades. You can earn a scholarship to college. This is money that is given to teens because their grade point average is either high, or a two point 0. I couldn't believe that I didn't tell my boys about this when they were younger. I wish I had of kept my grades up when I was younger, so that I could have a scholarship. I had a's and b's all the way up until high school. High school got a little hard, and then I got better at it. My last grade average for college was a three point 0. There are different companies that sponsor scholarships for teens, you just have to look on the web, or maybe call the company and find out. I'm talking about the big name companies. You can also watch the oakland district channel and they should have information.

There are different programs you can watch or send for on tv. There is the eyeQ program for speed reading. There is nickolodean magazine, the national readers digest and national word power challenge. The program info is at rd.com, it is for fourth through eigth grade. You can goto word power.com to play the game. The first prize is a 25,000 dollar college scholarship, 2nd prize is a 15,000 dollar scholarship, and 3rd prize is a 10,000 dollar scholarship. There is the Scripps Howard National Spelling Bee/Math Counts show. Math counts began in 1983. They have complex math problems and the children face off with each other. There is the PCA Pre Collegiate Academy Program at www.eastbayconsortium.com. There is a program called Project Soar, Chabot Science Center has a program, and there website is info@chabotspace.org. The

Oakland Public Library downtown has a section called "The teen zone." The Chavez Branch Library has the"Teen Section." There is the mayor summer job program that hires teens for different places like The Alameda county fair, Southwest airlines(must have high school diploma), Tunnese construction, YMCA, YEP(youth employment services program), the gap, old navy, and albertsons. You can watch the history, or the discovery channel too, to just feed your brain. There is the habitot childrens museum, which is great for adults to take their toddlers too, their website is www.habitot.com. Their is a quizkids championship show, at www.pentv.com. The children won a trip to Europe, or London, and a trophy. The losing team won 500 dollars. They have teen kids news on KRON 4. They have a garfield program on sleep deprivation. After the students complete the construction and architect academy, there is an internship for students. There are eight grade spelling finals held at the Oakland museum. The champion is announced on tv,given a trophy ,and has a photo taken.

For days upon hours I sat and watched tv. I tried to find another way for teens to have a reason to get an education. Martin Luther King, All the slaves that were massacred and mamed for reading would turn over in their grave with what's going on now. We as a black people have to get ourselves together, I say before we become extinct. We are to busy sueing,killing,talking about, discriminating against, putting down, abusing, rapeing, and degrading ourselves, to let anyone else do it. I know we are a proud people. We just have a lot going on in our lives. There is still modern day slavery that we are trying to handle. We are still trying to prove everyday that we are better than a lot of people on this earth. A lot of us really already have it going on. What I'm trying to say is how will we be able to figure out how to change the status in whcih we live in from day to day. To me our children are a very big part of it. Whatever it is that we cannot accomplish hopefully our children will. I know that's what all the other blacks before us felt. If the world is going to keep going round in circles for years to come when will we be on top as a people. When will we do something about it in a positive light. There have been times when I had to cry to myself over and over behind bills,food(not having any), being flat broke, dealing with my teens , and mom. I know that there are a lot of black people who have been worse off than I have, and I thank GOD everyday. There are only so many very rich people who give back to their communtiy, the home that they grew up in. Maybe if that started happening It would be better too. I know that people are helping over in Africa, but what about the poor right here in the United States. the only way most people deal with the economy(money situations) now is to move out of one area into another. We've got to find a peaceful way for our black economy to get better. Maybe then we will be looked at as higher citizens of the United States than what we are!

Thank you very much, for reading my book!

Traci

www.ingramcontent.com/pod-product-compliance
Lightning Source LLC
Chambersburg PA
CBHW020339290526
45785CB00005B/2090